Roots Out of Dry Ground

by

Reuben J. Swanson

Roots Out of Dry Ground

Reuben J. Swanson, S.T.M., Ph.D.
Professor of Philosophy and Religion
Western Carolina University
Cullowhee, North Carolina

WIPF & STOCK · Eugene, Oregon

Wipf and Stock Publishers
199 W 8th Ave, Suite 3
Eugene, OR 97401

Roots Out of Dry Ground
By Swanson, Reuben J.

Softcover ISBN-13: 978-1-7252-8778-5
Hardcover ISBN-13: 978-1-7252-8780-8
eBook ISBN-13: 978-1-7252-8779-2
Publication date 9/9/2020
Previously published by Western North Carolina Press, 1979

This edition is a scanned facsimile of the original edition published in 1979.

TO MARIAN

Helpmeet
and
inspiration

The author acknowledges with grateful appreciation the illustrations which have been prepared for this book by

Lee Budahl
The Art Department
Western Carolina University
Cullowhee, North Carolina

the encouragement, the suggestions, and kind words in the Preface by

John T. Bunn
Senior Minister
First Baptist Church
Sylva, North Carolina

as well as the many listeners in the pew who have been the subject and the object of this preaching over many years.

TABLE OF CONTENTS

To read this anthology of the sermons of Reuben Swanson is to once again become acquainted with a venerable and highly imaginative homiletical structure. Rarely does an ancient homiletical form rise to newness of life and convince the reader of its validity for contemporary preaching. Yet, just such a sermonic device will confront every possessor of this volume. The author has subconsciously retrieved and modernized the dramatic method of prophetic poetic prose, which is one of the most exacting of writing disciplines and of which the author is a past master. On first reading, one acquainted with Old Testament prophetic utterance, as found in Newer English translations, will note a similarity of style, movement and emphasis. Dr. Swanson is to be commended for restoring to preaching this exciting mode of proclamation.

Dr. John T. Bunn
Senior Minister
First Baptist Church
Sylva, N. C.

A MEDITATION ON ROOTS

EASTER, 1957

A ROOT OUT OF DRY GROUND

ISAIAH 53:2

A ROOT OUT OF A DRY GROUND

The joy of the Easter Season
    is the rebirth
    of spring
with all the color, the beauty,
    of living grass,
    of trees and flowers.
God so planned the resurrection
    of Jesus Christ
    that it coincides
with the coming to life
    of all nature.

There is no beauty
man can produce which compares
    to the beauty
    of living plants
    and of creatures—
the handiwork of God.

The beauty we see around us at Easter
    is the beauty
    of living flowers
    arrayed
    in their many colors.
But there is another beauty we see:
    the beauty
    of the smiling faces,
    of the shining eyes,
of the happy children of God.

The Root

We know
that just a short time ago
the Easter flowers
were only roots
in a dry ground.
They were roots laid to rest in the soil.
But through the mysterious workings
of life
which God had placed in them,
they came to life.
They pushed their way through the soil,
they grew up green and healthy.
They blossomed forth
in all their myriad colors
today.

We cannot fathom,
we cannot understand
the life power
which God placed
in these roots.
We cannot explain
why nature rests in this way
through the winter season,
only to burst forth to life
in the spring.

We only know
that this is part
of the mysterious working
of God.
These roots,
which only a short time ago
seemed dead,
are now alive.
This is a parable for us
of the way God works in us
through Jesus Christ.

The Root We Call Christ

In the prophet Isaiah we read,
"He grew up before him
like a young plant,
like a root
out of a dry ground."
This is symbolic,
this is figurative
of Jesus Christ.

When God sent his Son
to save us
from sin and death,
he did not send him
in the shining splendor
of God.
He came
clothed in human flesh,
disguised,
so that we could not recognize him
apart from faith.

Jesus grew up
like a root
out of a dry ground;
just as you and I grow up
from a tender root
to manhood
or womanhood.

We can compare the growth of Jesus
to one
of the Easter flowers today,
perhaps to an Easter lily,
or to the flower
most beautiful
to us.
This flower did not grow
without tender care,
without the right conditions
to make it a sturdy,
healthy,
beautiful plant.

Thus Jesus grew under the tender care
of Mary and Joseph
to whom God had entrusted
this tender plant.
He was nourished upon the food
which they had to offer,
so that his body grew to be
healthy and strong.
He was nurtured upon the scriptures,
upon the Word of God,
so that his inner life
of mind and spirit
blossomed forth in a beautiful life
of kindness and love.

The nature of God was in him.
He always acted in kindness and love,
so that he gave help,
he gave joy and peace,
to all who were around him.

When he grew to manhood,
he did not forsake God.
He knew that the only life,
    the life worth living,
    is the life
    in harmony with God.
His life was like a beautiful flower.
He brought the beauty of God's presence
    to the poor and sorrowful,
    to the anxious and troubled.

The flowers before us today live,
so that they might blossom forth
    in all their color and beauty
    to bring beauty and joy
    to the people of God.
Jesus lived on earth
in order to bring
    peace and joy,
    the beauty of God,
    into our lives.

He came to unite us
    into one family,
    the people of God,
so that we might grow up
and blossom forth
    into good, beautiful
    men and women,
showing forth in our lives
    the kindness and goodness,
    the humility and love,
which Jesus showed.

The Root Out Of A Dry Ground

Jesus was like a tender plant
before God.
But men did not love him.
They hated him
because his deeds
were good.
They crushed that tender plant!
They took him outside their city,
they nailed him
to a cross.
Most cruelly did they
put him
to death.

Those who loved him
took down
his broken body
from the cross.
Tenderly they dressed his wounds,
they anointed his broken body,
they laid him
in a tomb.

Then God worked the miracle of miracles,
a wonder so wonderful,
that words cannot express
the beauty, the marvel
of this story.
God awakened him to life again!
The root came forth
out of the dry ground.

His broken body was transformed!
He lives in a body more glorious,
    more beautiful,
    than any flower!
God clothed him in a glorious body,
    incorruptible,
    imperishable,
    immortal
    eternal.
Now he lives
    in all the shining splendor
    of heaven
    with God.

The Root Of Christ In Us

This is only the beginning
    of the story.
We too can be compared
    to the flower
    which grows forth
    like a root
out of a dry ground.

God intends that our lives too
    shall be beautiful,
    glorious,
like a pure white Easter lily.
God wants us to grow up before him
    like a tender plant,
    like a root
out of a dry ground.

He wants our lives to be
    unsullied,
    unstained
by sin and evil.
He wants us to be pure white
    in our transparency,
so that we do not let
    blackness,
    the smudge of sin,
besmirch our lives.

For this God sent his Son Jesus.
Sin and wickedness
    had blackened,
    had stained us.
We could not be clean
    even if we used
    all the world's cleansers.
The only way for us to be clean is
    to be forgiven
    by God.

He comes to purify us.
He comes to make us clean and pure
    like the beautiful,
    the white,
    Easter lily.
We are to be like Jesus!
We can be like him
    through God's love,
    through God's power.

When he forgives us,
when he plants faith
in our hearts,
he opens to us a new way,
a new life.
Now we are to keep ourselves
from uncleanness.
We are to be on guard against
the sins
which would make us
dirty and stained.

We are to restrain,
we are to overcome the impulses
to anger and hate,
to jealousy and envy,
to lying and stealing,
to swearing and impure thoughts,
to irreverence and disobedience to God.
When we permit these impulses
to fester,
to grow in us,
we stain and defile
the beautiful life
God has given to us.

We are followers of Jesus!
We are to become like him!
Sin is to be done away
in our lives!

Before the Easter lily became
the beautiful flower
we see today,
it was a root.
There was no beauty, no comeliness,
that we should
admire it.
But it was planted,
it grew,
it blossomed forth,
a thing of beauty which we behold.

Thus God plants
the root
of Jesus' life
in us.
When we are baptized into Christ,
we put on Christ.
His Spirit is planted
deep within us.
The Spirit of Christ lives,
The Spirit of Christ grows
in us,
as we are nurtured in God's Word,
as we fellowship,
as we live
among the people
of God.

As we live in Christ,
we become like him.
We are to do his deeds of kindness.
We are to be overflowing
with love
for one another.
This is the miracle of the new life!
God's Spirit is planted in us!
God's Spirit takes root and grows,
until we become
like Jesus
in this world.

But this is not all to our parable!
There is another chapter
    in our life story
    still to be written.
This earthly life is harsh and cruel.
    Strive as we might,
we never live up to the level
    of perfection
    we see in Jesus.

We yearn for the day
    when we will be complete.
We yearn for the heavenly life
    when we will be with God
    forever.
We have his promise,
    signed and sealed
    through the resurrection
    of Jesus,
that this will be true.

Some day our life on earth will come
    to an end.
We fear this experience!
It will be a day of tragedy,
    a day of evil,
    a most sorrowful experience
for each one of us.
But when the life of Jesus is in us,
    we do not fear
    that experience.
Rather,
we look forward
    to that event
    with eager longing.

For we know,
we believe what happened to Jesus
    when they put his body
    in the ground,
    will happen to us.
He was a root planted in a dry ground:
    a root which was dead,
    a root which came to life again.
For God raised him from the dead!

    This is the joy of Easter.
This is the message of this glad day.
    Though our bodies die,
    though our bodies decay to dust,
yet the root of life is there.
On the day of resurrection,
God will bring us forth
    from death,
    from the grave,
like a root out of a dry ground.

Our bodies will be changed!
We will be clothed in a new body,
    a body unsullied,
    a body unstained by sin,
    a body gloriously pure,
as clean and pure as the pure,
    white Easter lily.

Our bodies will be changed!
They will be as different
    from our present bodies
as the beautiful Easter lily
in all its shining splendor is different
    from the root planted
    in a dry ground.

We will be clothed in a new body!
A body like Christ's resurrection body—
    incorruptible,
    imperishable,
    immortal,
    eternal,
    glorious!
Then the life which God plants in us now,
    will have reached
    its full growth.
Then God's purpose
will be fully realized
    in us.

For then a root has grown
    out of a dry ground,
    a beautiful plant
which will always flourish
    and flower
    in God's heaven.

A MEDITATION ON WITNESS

THE THIRD SUNDAY IN ADVENT, 1978

A TESTIMONY TO JESUS

JOHN 1.6-8, 19-28

A TESTIMONY TO JESUS

The testimony of a witness
can be
very compelling.
Many a case at law has been decided
by a witness
whose testimony
had the ring of truth.

In many other situations in life
our course of action,
our very life,
can be fashioned by the testimony
of a witness
to his convictions,
to his ideals.

We can be deeply moved
by the orator,
by the teacher,
by the statesman,
yes, even
by the politician.
We can be lifted out of ourselves
to follow a calling,
a way of life,
an ideal
presented
in a new, a powerful way.

John was a Witness

Our lesson today is
	about a witness,
	a man
who gave testimony to another,
	to one
	whom he did not know.
	"He comes after me,"
he said,
	"the thong of his sandal
	I am not worthy to untie."

There is something unique
	about this witness,
He did not come to tell
	about himself.
He did not come to gain
	a following.
He did not come to begin
	a new religious movement.
He came out of the past,
but he pointed to the future.
	Out of the past
	for he recalled
	the ancient prophet,
	Elijah,
in his zeal, his enthusiasm, for God.
He proclaimed a message,
	not different
from the great prophets of old:
	"Repent!
	Turn to God!
The judgment of God is at hand!
The end of the age is near!
	Prepare for the coming
	of the Lord!
God will visit his people!"

He also pointed to the future,
to the Coming One.
To the One
he believed God was even now
raising up
to usher in
the great, the wonderful day,
of the Lord.
"He stands among you,"
he said,
"but you do not know him."

What an unusual witness!
"Who are you?"
asked the priests
sent to him from Jerusalem.
"I am not the Christ,"
he said.

Who is the Christ?
The expected One.
God had promised his people,
"In the latter days
I will send my Anointed."
Those days had all the marks
of the last days.
There was gross wickedness,
evil,
in the land.
Selfishness and greed ruled
in the hearts
of men.
God's people were oppressed,
dominated,
by a powerful foreign power.

For ages they had looked
        for a deliverer,
        for the Anointed
        of God.
He would loose them from foreign rule,
        set them free,
        to fulfill
        their destiny
as the chosen people of God.

There was great expectation
        among the people.
They had a sixth sense
        that the day
        of deliverance
was about to dawn upon them.
This man in the wilderness,
        with his powerful message,
        with his zeal,
        his fervor for God,
had the marks of the Anointed!
        they thought.

They came to him.
      "Who are you?"
they said.
      "are you the Christ?
        the Anointed?"
How tempting to say, "Yes!"
For personal ambition seeks
        a following,
        a power base,
        the honor,
        the glory of men.
Why be a witness,
unless one is able to mold,
to shape the people
        into a hero cult?

But this witness replied,
"No!
I am not the Christ."
Then they asked,
"Who are you then?
Are you Elijah?"
He had all the marks of Elijah,
that great prophet of old.
He appeared in the wilderness,
dressed in a robe of camel's hair,
eating locusts and wild honey,
proclaiming with zeal and fervor
the demands of God upon his people.

There was a tradition,
long held
by the people,
that in the last days
Elijah
would return.
That this mighty prophet of old
would rise up
to announce
the day of the Lord.

Elijah
had not died.
He had been taken in a fiery chariot
into heaven
to await
the strategic moment to return
to earth.

How tempting for John to say,
"I am Elijah."
The people would have flocked to him.
They would have idolized him.
What power
he could have commanded!
Why, he could even qualify
as the Anointed of God!
Who would know the difference?

Many people long for a leader,
even a religious leader,
who will lead them
into the promised land,
into the Garden of Eden.
How many there are
who are willing to be deceived
by the clever,
by the manipulator.
How tempting it is
to be that kind of person
when the conditions
are right.

But John was a witness,
He said,
"I am the voice
of one crying
in the wilderness,
'Make straight the way of the Lord.'"
Only a voice,
but a powerful spokesman
for God!

The Testimony

John came for testimony,
    to bear witness
    to the light.
He was not the light,
But came to bear witness
    to the light.
Light and darkness are
two descriptive words to describe
    the status,
    the condition,
    of men.

    There is darkness!
But in the beginning God said,
    "Let there be light!"
    And there was light.
Light and darkness are as different
    as night from day.
    Lost in the night,
we have known darkness:
    the fear,
    the panic,
from the sounds we cannot see,
    but only hear.

    Darkness is black!
A symbol of sin and evil.
    Light is white!
    The symbol of righteousness,
    of purity.
When it is light, who needs
    to bear witness
    to the light?
Cannot we see the light?
Do we need a witness to point
    to the light?

Yes!
When darkness is the spiritual state,
        the condition,
        of our hearts.
For those who are bound fast
        in the chains
        of sin
know not the light.
They grope in the dark,
        stumbling and falling,
        overwhelmed
        by fear and terror
at the sounds of the night.

But an even worse condition prevails
        among many children
        of men.
We may believe that we are in the light,
that we can see,
        but be in darkness
        nevertheless.
For sin and evil have a way of masking,
        of blindfolding,
        our eyes,
We see,
        but not the light of God.

We see.
But we walk in darkness
        whenever we walk not
        in the ways of God.
Whenever self and selfishness,
whenever greed and lust,
whenever pleasure and the love
        of the things
        of the world
        rule our hearts,
we walk in darkness.
We do not know the light.

John came to bear witness
to the light.
He came to a people
who believed
that they knew the light.
They were certain that they were
in the ways of God.
How deceived we can be!
How we can substitute for God,
worshiping imitations,
with no awareness
of the dreadful darkness
that rules our hearts.

People were curious
about the witness of John.
They heard as far away as Jerusalem
of this new preacher
who had appeared
in the wilderness.
They sent their representatives
to check him out.
To determine
how authentic was his message.

After all, there is an official religion.
One that is time honored.
With its cult representatives
who believe
that they have the last word
from God.
Who iook with scornful eyes
upon the freelancer,
the prophet,
whose credentials are only his own claim.

"Who are you?"
they said.
"Why do you baptize,
if you are neither the Christ,
nor Elijah,
nor the prophet?"
Who has given you this authority?

Perhaps there was some name calling
which has dropped
from the record.
For we have choice,
descriptive words
for those
who come as messengers of light,
but whose claims we do not want
to recognize.

But John would not be swayed
either by the acclaim
of the people
or by the intimidations
of the priestly hierarchy.
He cried,
"I am the voice of one
crying in the wilderness,
'Make straight the way of the Lord.'"

The One Coming

Our season,
the times,
the word of God—
all proclaim with one voice:
"There is one
among you
whom you do not know."

For who knows the Coming One?
Who is looking for the Savior
of the world?
We are looking for many things this season:
for fun and pleasure,
for treasure and security,
for honor and power.
We may even be looking for salvation.
But salvation from what?
or to what?

Mostly we are looking for salvation
from our sicknesses,
from our ailments.
We are looking for salvation
from our debts,
from our obligations.
We are looking for salvation
from boredom,
from meaninglessness in life.

Why are so many willing to go out
into the wilderness
following a prophet
whom they do not know?
the Moonies,
the Peoples' Church,
the Hare Krishnas.
Do these prophets have the light,
the light of God?
Are they the saviors they claim
themselves to be?
Can they rid the world of darkness?

There is one among us
whom we do not know.
He comes quietly,
so shrouded in human form
that we do not recognize him
as coming from God.
We look for greatness in the One
from God.
The One who can stir multitudes.
The One who can lead the people
out of the wilderness,
into the promised land.

But the mystery of God is great!
He is shrouded in human form,
so that human eyes
cannot behold him.
Those who walk in darkness
are not impressed.
They have their illusions of grandeur
which to them
are for real.

Surely God can do better than to come
    in a little infant,
    born of human parents,
    sheltered by a stable
    with a manger for a crib.
Surely the light of God should be
    so bright
that we cannot mistake him
    at his coming.

    How quietly,
    how silently,
the gift of God is given.
    The gift
that can lead us out of darkness
    into light.
    He comes!
    But he is here!
John came to bear witness to the light.
He was not the light,
    but came to bear witness
    to the light,
that all might believe through him.

    The gift of faith,
    the gift of sight,
is offered to all who hear
    the testimony
    of the witness.
To all who with great searchings
    of heart
    come out of the darkness
to walk in the light.

For the gospel,
the witness to Jesus Christ,
is the great searchlight
which lays bare
the secrets
of our hearts.
Which uncovers the selfish motives
that have ruled
and dominated
our lives.
Which points up to us that we walk
in the way of darkness,
in the way of death,
when we walk not
in the ways of God.

There is one who bears witness
to the light.
His testimony is:
"Among you stands one
whom you do not know,
even he who comes
after me."

The true witness points
to this one,
unknown and nameless,
who comes among us.
Who comes to deliver us,
to free us,
from darkness
and evil.
Who comes to present us to God—
to the God
of truth and light
that we might forever
belong to him.

Behold!
He is coming!
Behold!
He is here!
He is none other
than Jesus Christ
our Lord!

A MEDITATION ON THIRST

THE SECOND SUNDAY IN LENT, 1975

WITHOUT A DRINK OF WATER

John 4.5-26

WITHOUT A DRINK OF WATER

The bright, shining sun,
The burning wind,
The dusty road.
Have you ever been so thirsty
that your flesh cried out
for a drink of water?
Cool, cool water?

To be without water can be
a most excruciating
experience.
Jesus craved the cooling water too.
He sat by the well,
but he had nothing
to draw up
the water.

Coleridge describes such a situation
in "The Rime of the Ancient Mariner":
"Water,
water everywhere,
and not a drop to drink."

Physical Thirst

We have all known physical thirst.
And hunger too!
We are mostly warmed and fed,
    but we have experienced
    hunger and thirst.
The thirst for water is
    but one of the many
    thirsts of man.

Our thirst for things can be
    a consuming fire.
How we American people long
    for things!
We have an abundance,
    but an abundance
    is all too few.

There is no comparison
    of our way of life
    to the ways
    of many peoples
    of the earth.
There is poverty.
There is thirst:
    thirst
    for the essentials
    of life—
like a drink of cooling water.

The drought in a great belt
across the heart of equatorial Africa
    has brought
    the most frightful thirst
    to many.
The story is pitiful:
    starving men,
    starving beasts.
    Starving
because the cooling drink of water
    has not fallen
    from the heavens
    upon the parched earth beneath.

God has spared us from such tragedy.
    But are we grateful?
Why are we so reluctant to share
    a cup of cold water
    with the thirsty?
    a morsel of bread
    with the hungry?
The sin of having plenty is not
    in having plenty.
No!
The sin of having plenty rises
    when we do not share
    with those
    who have not.

Thirst can be a spiritual disease!
When we are so in love with things
    that things are more important
    than people,
    than we have sinned!
Than we give expression
    to the fatal selfishness
    at the base of our being.

Thirst robs us of God
when it is a thirst
for things.
When we place the priority
on all the things
that we possess.
Jesus said,
"What shall it profit a man
if he gains the whole world
and forfeits his own life?"

But we have not taken him seriously,
have we?
Is it not more important to have things
than to be in a right,
a true relationship,
with God?
For when we are in a right,
a true relationship,
with God,
we are in a right, a true relationship,
with one another.

What is the cause of anger,
of hatred and jealousy,
of envy and strife,
of malice and bitterness?
Is it not our thirst for things?
We are at the well,
but the well is deep
and we have nothing
with which to draw.

Where can we find the living water
which will assuage our thirst
forever?
The mountain streams run
swift and cool.
But even they
cannot cool
our parched tongues.
Not when our thirst
is truly
for the living God.

Spiritual Thirst

Spiritual thirst
is more terrible
than any physical thirst
we may exerience.
To be like Job,
to search for the living God,
and not find him!

The soul crying out in vain
for the living God
suffers
the very agonies of a burning hell.
Jeremiah speaks of a burning fire
"shut up in my bones
and I cannot be silent."
The Psalmist speaks of the hart panting
for cooling streams:
"So pants my soul for you,"
he says,
"for the living God."

Yes!
Our real problem is spiritual.
We mask and cover up
    our need for God
    by the multiplication
    of things!
Jesus knew of that kind of thirst too.
He sensed it in people—
    that dreadful thirst,
    that drives us
    into the most gross acts
    of idolatry and sin.

There was the woman at the well.
What kind of woman is this who comes
    to draw water
    in the heat of the day?
Does she have something to hide
from the prying eyes of neighbor?
    Does she dread
    the unkind remarks
    of the righteous?

Yes!
She has been busy with her things.
She has followed
    the way
    of wickedness and shame!
She has had five husbands
and the man she now lives with
    is not her husband!
The new and novel ways of some today
    are not so new and novel
    after all.

No!
Mankind and womankind have changed very little
    over some tens of thousands of decades.
There are
    the same desires,
    the same thirsts,
    the same drives,
fragmenting us in the midst of mankind.
Foreclosing to us the possibilities
    of true and loving relationships
    with one another.

Why can we not be at peace with one another?
Why can we not be kind to one another?
Why can we not be helpful to one another?
    Are these attitudes and actions
    born of God?
Is God selfish?
Is God unkind?
Is God unloving?

Why is it so impossible to humble ourselves?
To admit our errors and our sins?
To acknowledge that we have sinned against one another?
    Is it not the selfish ego
    at the heart of each one of us?
rather than God,
    that drives us to such gross acts
    against one another?

What is it to be gross?
Is it to live in open immorality?
Is it to be boastfully defiant of God?
    No,
    not entirely!
It is gross to treat any person
    made in the image of God,
    as we ourselves are,
as though he or she were a thing!

Yes!
We thirst for the living God.
"Where can I find him?"
cried Job.
But we have covered our thirst
with a multitude of things,
little realizing
or caring
that this is the way of death.

The Encounter With Jesus

But one sits at the well
by the side of the road.
Our pathway
crosses his pathway.
His look is penetrating.
His questions incisive.
He sees through us:
through the sham and shallowness
that is our shield
against truth and against God.

"Where can I find him?"
cried the woman at the well.
"Not in this mountain,
not even in Jerusalem,"
said Jesus.
He is here!
In this moment of time
when our innermost self
is laid bare
before the living God.

Where is this water,
this living water,
      that quenches
      our thirst forever?
Is it not here in this man Jesus?
This man by the side of the road?
This man with outstretched hand,
      with inviting eye?

Does he not call us too
      from the fleshpots
      of this world?
Does he not call us,
    "Come to me
      all who labor
      and are heavy laden?"
Yes! He calls!
      His invitation goes forth
      to all the earth.

Even this woman by the well,
      stained and sullied
      by a life of sin,
is not beyond his call.
No!
His invitation is for all of us.
      For rich and for poor,
      for wise and for fools,
      for sinners and for righteous too!

But here is our problem.
We are not the woman by the well.
We have lived comfortable,
      though stodgy,
      righteous lives.
We are good enough for God,
      the way we are,
      are we not?

What joy!
What peace!
What glory!
Grabbed the woman at the well that day.
"Oh, that I might know him,"
she cried.
"Where can I find him?"
What joy in this story.

We have searched,
we have strained,
for that cooling water
that will slake our thirst.
We have run here and there.
We have searched high and low.
We have given and spent,
only to find that our thirst
is even more burning
than it was before!

No!
We do not find him, the One
Who is the answer to our quest.
We have not the power to run to God!
He is beyond our reach.
He is holy!
He is majestic!
He is sovereign
of heaven and earth!

But he waits by the side of the road.
He meets us at the point of
our deepest need.
He runs us to earth,
we who would flee
from God.

And he calls us!
He invites us
    to drink of the water
that will quench our thirst forever,
    of the living water
    of the cooling water.
For here we are without a drink of water.

But there is a stream, a living stream,
    that flows
    from the heart of God.
It is a cooling stream.
It is a life-giving well.
It is none other than
    the one by the side of the road,
    the one who waits by the well.
He is the living water:
    He quenches our thirst.
    He ends our quest for peace.
    He gives meaning to our lives.
    He gives purpose
which rises above the claims of self.

Yes,
He calls us!
He quenches our thirst!
But only to send us forth in his name
    to offer cooling water
    to those who are
    without a drink of water.
For his water is a mighty stream.
When we drink of his water,
we cannot be the same.
    Our will,
    our desire,
    our thirst,
is now for the lives of men.

We see the thirsty, the needy,
    drawing near
    to draw
from the watering troughs all about us;
    drawing water that cannot
    quench their thirst.
we see them, and we know them,
    for we have been
    to these wells before them.

We too have drunk of the water
    that cannot satisfy.
We too have eaten of the bread
    that cannot sate
    our hunger for God.

But no more!
For now our lives have become
    a flowing stream,
    drawing water
from the deep wells of the heart of God.
    What wonder!
    What glory!
That God calls us to share
    this everflowing stream
    with those at the well
without a drink of water.

A MEDITATION ON GETHSEMANE

LENT, 1958

I WAS THERE IN GETHSEMANE

Mark 14. 32-42

I WAS THERE IN GETHSEMANE

I was there that night
Jesus suffered agony
in Gethsemane.

I saw the little group of men
with Jesus in the lead
wend their way through
the narrow streets
of Jerusalem.

I saw them pass through the gates
leading out of the city.
I heard the challenge
of the watchman on duty.
I saw the darkened city
sleeping peacefully,
unaware of the tragedy
which even now was unfolding.

I saw here and there
a flickering light,
now flashing up
perhaps as a mother rose up
to comfort her child in distress;
then going out like a firefly
as the basket was again placed
over the lampstand.

I saw the silent olive trees
      making their silhouettes in the moonlight,
      standing like sentries along the darkened way.
I heard the wind
      whispering in the leaves,
      telling the secrets of the night.
I heard the footfalls of the travelers
      as they mounted the path
      to the summit of the hill.

I heard the voices of the disciples,
      wondering in muted tones,
      'Why this excursion into the night
      at this late hour?'
I saw the look of determination,
      of anticipation,
      yes, even of anxiety and dread,
      upon the face of the man in the lead.

I was there!
But I did not realize
      the meaning of that hour.
I did not understand
      the 'why' of Gethsemane.
I did not comprehend the prayer
      my Savior prayed that night.
I did not understand his words.
My eyes were heavy
      for the hour was late.
My mind was dull from the excitement of Jerusalem—
      the many pilgrims,
      the hurried preparations
      for the holy feast of Passover
      and Unleavened Bread.

THE GARDEN

We came to the garden,
A familiar spot,
for we had often gathered here
with the Master.
It was a quiet place,
secluded,
hidden from the view
of the travelers on the way.

I remember how the Master
talked about the things of God
in this place.
My mind goes back to his words
about love for God
and love for neighbor.
Words about trust in the mercies of God.
Words about hope for the life to come.

He spoke of purity and goodness,
of true joy and peace.
I remember how he promised forgiveness,
the grace of God
to the prodigal.
My heart goes back to that place,
to the quietness
the contentment we loved
away from the cares,
the troubles of the world.

I was there that night.
Now i understand the agony,
the intensity of the Master's prayer,
his pleading with his Father,
his remonstrance to his sleeping companions.
Now I know why he prayed three times
with increasing fervor.
I saw him with his face upon the ground
as he pleaded with his Father.
I remember how he said,
"Pray that you may not enter
into temptation."

The Temptation

I know our Savior was tempted
    in every way
    as we are tempted.
Tempted to rebel against the will of God.
Tempted to go his own way,
Tempted to turn back from stern duty
    from a fearful cross.

I was there!
I saw him wrestle
    with the powers of evil.
I saw him grovel on the ground
    in the agony of the fearful struggle.
I believe
    that Jesus Christ is true God and true man.
    My God and my brother.
He is my God.
    He came forth from the Father.
    He is from all eternity.
    He was with the Father
    Before the creation of the world.
    He is my Lord, my God.

But he is also my brother,
    bone of my bone
    flesh of my flesh.
For he was born of the Virgin.
He grew to manhood as we grow and mature.
He was human
    in all his needs and desires.
I saw him in Gethsemane.
    I know how human he was
    in the hour of temptation.

How oft in life we are tempted
to go our own way!
To turn our backs upon God.
To turn back from the duties,
the responsibilities,
of the godly life.
How thoughtless I would be
if I had not been
to Gethsemane that night!
How careless I would be
if I had not heard him pray
pleading with power
with his face to the ground.

Now when we are tempted,
we can go to Gethesemane.
There we see the fearful power of evil.
We behold our God and our brother
praying for us
before the throne of grace.
We hear again his word,
"Pray that you may not enter
into temptation."

I was there!
But I must return again and again
to Gethsemane.
I must be reminded
of the fierce power of evil.
I must lay hold
on the power of God
to strengthen me
in this awful struggle.

I must know in my heart that God loves
when I hear him pray:
"Abba, Father,
all things are possible to you;
remove this cup from me;
yet not what I will,
but what you will."

The Prayer

What does he mean by these words?
Why does he invoke the power of God?
    What is this cup
    about which he prays?
How can this quiet garden,
The dozing watchers
    create this atmosphere
    of tension and struggle?
I was there!
But I did not understand.

Now I have come to realize
the reason for Gethsemane
    for I stand
    under the shadow
    of the cross.
Jesus foreknew the power,
    the agony,
    the suffering
    of the Cross
in that dark hour in Gethsemane.

He was tempted to turn away from the Cross,
to take an easier way,
    to compromise
    with his enemies,
    with the powers of evil.
Surely God could spare him the Cross!
For all things are possible to God.
    Could not God
    forgive our sins,
    save us for eternal life
without this brutal death?

I once thought sin was not so bad,
just a blemish easily erased.
    But now I know
    the dark,
    deep power of evil.
For I was there that night!

Evil is not a blemish,
a spot,
marked
by the little wrongs
we do.
Evil is the mind,
the heart,
the will
of man against God.

Evil is a power that holds us
in bondage.
The power of evil brings us down
to sin and death. There is no escape:
we are all human,
we all share
in this rebellion of heart
and mind
and will
of man against God.

God wrestled with the powers of evil
in the garden
that night!
God was on the ground
in that fearful struggle
for the souls of men!
The Son of God pleaded with the Father
to bring all his powers
to bear against the evil powers
which were thrusting this fearful Cross
upon him.

He said to his disciples,
"My soul
is very sorrowful,
even to death."
Do you know that he is God?
Do you perceive the perfection,
the purity,
of his person?
Do you know that he is holy,
without sin?
Can you comprehend the revulsion
of his spirit
at the thought
of this dark stain upon himself?

God was on the ground!
But it was not the earth's dust
which stained him
causing his agony
of spirit!
The Lamb of God was bearing
the sin of the world.
The Son of God was drinking
the cup of death and hell
to free us
from this bitter end.

The black shadow of death
overshadowed him,
crushed him to the ground,
in this fearful struggle
with the powers of evil.
I was there!
I know the price the Son of God
paid to gain
our peace of heart.
I know the bitter cup
he drank
to rescue
us from hell!

The Victory

Three times he prayed that prayer:
"Father,
all things are possible
to you.
Remove this cup from me;
yet not what I will,
but what you will."
Three times he pleaded for release.
Three times the answer was the same:
"There is no other way.
The cup must be drained
To the last bitter drop."

I was there!
I saw him with his face
upon the ground,
struggling
with his decision.
I sensed the fearful agony
of mind
and spirit.
Now I know our salvation weighed
in the balance
that night.
Our destiny rested with him
in the garden.

He was true to himself
He was true to his Father.
He was true to his purpose
for coming
into the world.

He said,
"Now is my soul troubled.
And what shall I say,
'Father,
save me from this hour'?
No!
for this purpose
I have come to this hour.
Glorify thy Son
that thy Son
may glorify thee."

God was on the ground that night!
He prayed.
He pleaded
with his Father in his hour
of temptation.
But he rose up from the ground!
He went with firm step,
with resolute will
with peace in his heart
to take the place of all mankind
in this death
for sin.

He rose up triumphant,
victorious,
over the hosts of evil.
He rose up,
not as the conquered,
but as the conqueror.
He bore in silence,
with patience,
the cruelty,
the injustice of men,
because he had been to Gethsemane
with God.

There is a Gethsemane for every one of us.
There is a place of prayer
where we go
to meet our God.
I know, for I was there!

When beset by the tempter's power,
when rent and torn by selfish desire,
when overcome by the cares,
    the anxieties,
    of life,
I go back to Gethsemane.

I review once more
    the meaning
    of this hour.
When I am on the ground,
he lifts me up!

I go to Gethsemane to find
    my faith reborn,
    my hope rekindled,
    my love renewed.
Ah, those precious moments
    in Gethsemane,
when all the power of God
    is brought to bear
    upon my need.

I have found we cannot walk
    the way of life
    alone.
We cannot meet temptation,
We cannot overcome ourselves,
We cannot take up our cross,
We cannot follow him
    until we have been
    to Gethsemane.
I was in the garden that night!
    but I go back
    again and again.

There is a Gethsemane for you.
If you have never been there,
Come,
Let us rise
And go!
We will never understand the saving mission
of the Son of God
until we have been
to Gethsemane with him.

We will never know the duty,
the calling,
of the Christian life,
Until God has formed
and molded
and shaped
our minds and our hearts
in Gethsemane.

Here the purpose of God becomes
crystal clear.
Here we learn the way
of God to man.
Here we find the way
from man to God
I know! For I was there
in Gethsemane
that night.

A MEDITATION
ON THE RESURRECTION

EASTER, 1978

THE STONE WAS ROLLED AWAY

Matthew 28. 1-10

THE STONE WAS ROLLED AWAY

Stones!
Great stones!
Small stones!
Heaps of stone!
Stone cliffs!
Stone mountains!
Cutting stones!
Grinding stones!
Building stones!
A stone of stumbling and a rock of offense.
A corner stone!
Stones to sit upon!
Stones to throw at sinners!
AND THE STONE WAS ROLLED AWAY!
When Jesus was crucified,
when he died,
they took his body down from the cross,
they laid it in a tomb,
newly hewn from stone.
Then they rolled a great stone over the tomb
and went away.
When the women came to the tomb
the first day of the week,
they wondered,
"Who will roll away the stone from the tomb?"

And an angel descended
    and rolled back the stone
    and sat upon it;
A stone which some ancient versions say
Was so large that scarcely twenty men could move it.

The Bible is full of stones.
Our lives are full of stones.
But the stone which has the most meaning of all for us
    is the stone that was rolled away.

The Tombstone

    Life ends at the grave.
Those who buried the body of Jesus
Never expected to see him again.
    This was the end.

They carried out their respects to the dead
    with sorrow.
They had expected so much from Jesus.
He had opened a future
    of promise and hope.

But all this came to an end
    as they wrapped his body in linen
    and rolled the stone over the tomb
    and went away.

They thought of Sheol,
    a dark and shadowy place,
    not the abode of the dead;
But the place of the dead where they went
    never to return.

Have we not stood at the grave?
Have we not said,
    "This is it!"
Have we not mourned and lamented
    the passing of our loved ones?

Have we not placed the stone over the tomb
    and gone away?
Have we not carried our grief
    for days and weeks,
    even for years?
Yes, the graveyard is a solemn place.
A place for melancholy thoughts.

There are the stones,
    the hard stones,
    the unfeeling stones.
The stones carved with the names of those we love
The stones marking the resting place
    of our dreams and hopes,
    of our very life.

Throughout the ages mankind has lived
    in the shadow of the stones,
    knowing that his life is brief.
Knowing that only a stone
    marks his final resting place.

The life of Jesus came to an end
His place too was marked by a stone,
    a great stone,
which with great effort
    was rolled over the tomb.

The Stone Rolled Over the Tomb

There is an eternity to the stones.
We speak of the everlasting hills,
    the stones which are always with us,
    the stones which mark our final restingplace.

But even stones are not eternal.
They erode and wear away to dust
    over the eons of time.
They become the dust out of which our bodies
    are shaped and formed.

From dust we are and to dust we shall return.
    Shaped and molded
    of the dust of the age-old stones.
What can life be but a shadow?
What can life be but mortal?
Are not the stones more powerful
    than flesh and blood?

When we look at the enduring stones,
    what is man?
    what is he but mortal?
Born into a world of sorrow and trouble.
Struggling to survive.
Struggling to carve out a niche for himself,
    a niche soon covered over
    by the sands of time.

How strange!
That in the course of the eons of time
    the great stones become dust,
    silent, dead dust.
Dust, blown about and settling
    we know not where.

But by the mighty power of God
That dust becomes
    living tissue,
    flesh and blood and nerve,
A living being.

We are given life by the power of God.
For he formed our bodies
    out of the dust of the ground.
He breathed into our nostrils
    the breath of life
    and we came alive.

Did we come alive only to die?
Were we created
    only for the moment?
Only for the fleeting time
    we call a life?

No!
We were created to enter into fellowship
    with our Creator.
To partake of his eternal nature.
    To live and die.
    To live again.

For sin entered into the world.
The living dust did not keep its place
    in obedience to God.
Man turned from serving God
    to seek his own.
    to serve himself.

Thus the mold was broken.
The living tissue of mind, body, spirit
    was reduced to dust once more.
Death came,
The eternal lot of all those
    who fail to live up to the high promise
    of the Creator God.

How tragic!
How futile the promise of life!
    Born to die!
Created of dust,
Reduced to dust in the end.
Born of stone and reduced
    to stone with
    the passage of time.

A stone marks the end.
For a great stone was rolled over the tomb
and they went away.
Out of the dust he came.
To dust he returns again
Held deep in the earth by the great stone
which covered him.

The Rolled Away Stone

But that stone did not hold
its victim.
Jesus Christ came forth from the grave
with a mighty shout!
The stone was rolled away.

The tomb was opened.
The dead man was raised to life
by the power of God.
The power of death and the grave
was forever broken.
God the Creator of life,
God who molded his Son out of
the dust of the ground,
Is the Lord of life and death.

What is dust?
or earth?
or stone?
But the artifact of God?
How is it that he can shape living tissue
out of dead matter?
And when living tissue becomes dead matter,
is it forever dead?

Not when the will of God is exercised
to create life out of death.
For he spoke and it was so.
He commanded and it was done.
The dead came to life.
The dust became living tissue.

But not tissue of flesh and blood,
For a new being,
    a heavenly, spiritual being
    was born.

In that mighty act of God
    the stone was rolled away.
That stone which held relentless power over
    the feeble strength of man
    was crushed to dust.
And that dust was fashioned and molded
    into life;
Into an immortal, glorious, heavenly being.

Jesus Christ was raised from the dead
    by the mighty power of God!
He lives: the Lord of life!
That is the glorious message
    of this day.

No longer do we need to stand
before the relentless earth
that opens wide
    to receive the dust
    that once was man.
The power of death is forever broken
    by him who died
    to free us from its power.

We worship a living Lord,
One who tasted death
    for every man.
One who experienced every human weakness and woe.
One who came from God to shape and mold us
    into living, spiritual beings,
    inbreathed with the breath of God.

We too are shaped out of the dust of the ground;
Out of the dust that once was stone,
    hard, enduring stone.
In the providence of God,
By his skillful creative power,
    we became living beings.
Living beings with
    thought, motion, sensation,
    remembrance and love.

Sometimes we are too much like the stone
    out of which we were born.
There is a hardness, a resistance,
    not like living tissue,
    but more like the enduring stone
    out of which we are shaped.

This is our sin:
    to withstand our Creator
    to become like stone against him.
To resist the impulses for
    goodness and love,
    truth and generosity.
To deny the Creator God:
To deny love and forgiveness
    which he freely offers.

Yes, we are trapped in the grave
    which we have dug.
A grave walled with the stones,
    The sins we have done.
Unable to break free.
Destined to return to the dust
    from which we have sprung.

But God would not have it!
He comes in love and mercy.
He comes in his Son Jesus.
He comes to rescue us,
    to free us,
    from our entombment.

The stone that held us is rolled away.
Jesus Christ is raised from the dust,
    from the grave.
We are forever free!
But no! We must have him,
    for the stone remains
    until he comes.
We cannot by our own strength roll away
    the stone that holds us.

It is in his power,
In the power of God that
    the stone is rolled away.
We are raised from the dead,
From the deadness of sin and evil,
    to live with God
    and with one another.

O death where is your victory?
O death where is your sting?
The power of death is overthrown by him
    who has conquered death,
    who lives forevermore!
No longer do we walk in dread of death,
    we are at peace,
    we who trust in God.

Yes!
The stone has been forever rolled away.
But has it been rolled away
    from our lives?
Are we still bound up
    in the fleshly life of dust?
Is there a stone, a great stone,
    a mountain of sin,
    separating us from God?

Do we prefer the stone,
the stone that covers us
to God?
For we can never be at peace
with God and man
Until the stone is rolled away
from our lives.
The stone that separates us from God.
The stone that marks our fierce rebellion
against God.
The stone of selfishness,
of self-centeredness,
of pride and self-will.

Easter is the end of the old life
of sin and death.
For the stone is rolled away.
All that separated us from God,
from life,
from peace, joy, love
has been rolled away in Christ.

Easter is the beginning of the new life
of forgiveness,
of salvation.
The beginning of peace, joy, love.
God has forever rolled away the stone.

Has he rolled the stone away
from our hearts?
Are we at peace with him and with every man
because Christ rose up from the grave?
Today he renews his eternal gift to us
through his word.
Today he reminds us
once more:
THE STONE HAS BEEN ROLLED AWAY.

A MEDITATION ON ANXIETY

THE THIRD SUNDAY AFTER EASTER
1970

WHY ARE YOU ANXIOUS AND TROUBLED?

John 16. 16-22

WHY ARE YOU ANXIOUS AND TROUBLED?

Jesus said
to his disciples,
"Why are you anxious and troubled?
Why are you afraid?"
He was saying,
What do you have to worry about?

His disciples were normal men
for their time.
They must have been strong men
physically
and emotionally.
But they were very human.
They were oppressed
by nameless fears,
by anxieties.
Jesus found it necessary to point out
that their fears
and anxieties
were mostly groundless.

His answer to fears and anxieties was:
Trust in God
who has created you.
Believe in him!
He cares for you.
Does Jesus need to say
to us today,
"Why are you anxious and troubled?
Why are you afraid?"
Yes!
We need this word
from our Lord,
for we are an anxious people.

We can drum up more things
to fear,
to be anxious about,
than there are things.
In yesterday's paper a man was quoted,
saying,
He was so worried about whether or not
the astronauts would return safely
that he developed
an ulcer.

Fears from Without

If I had the power
to look
into your minds and hearts
to see you
as you really are,
I would see all kinds
of anxieties
and fears.

Jesus spoke
about one kind
of anxiety
when he said,
"Do not be anxious about your life,
what you shall eat or
what you shall drink,
nor about your body,
what you shall put on."

Some of us are anxious
about food
and drink
and clothing.
This word from Jesus is very
relevant.
When Jesus
spoke these words
to the people of his time,
he spoke to people who were fearful
because they did not have enough
to eat,
to drink,
or to wear.

That is not our problem.
We have plenty
to eat,
to drink,
and to wear.
In fact, we have too much.
And we worry because we have
too much.
Since we eat and drink too much,
we worry
about being overweight,
or about cholesterol,
or about heart attacks.
Thus we cannot, we do not have,
joy in the food
and drink
which God so abundantly provides.

We give thanks to God
    when we eat
    and drink.
Then we worry because he has given us
    too much.
There are many people in the world
    who would like
    to have our problem
about eating and drinking rather than
    their own.
Many do not have enough to eat.
And for the most part we do not care.
    The scraps
    from our tables
    which go into the garbage
have more calories than a full day's supply
    for the majority
    of the world's population.

Some of us worried about what
    we should wear
    as we dressed
    for church today.
But our problem was not
    an insufficiency,
    but an oversufficiency.
It would never do to come into the presence
    of the Lord
    twice
    in the same outfit.

We worried more about what we looked like
    on the outside
    than whether or not
    our inner person
    was in good shape
to appear before the living God.

God is not impressed by what
we wear.
Although it may well be
our neighbor is.
Thus we dress to please men.
But did we come out today to appear
before men?
or before God?
Often we suffer from such misplaced
priorities.

Jesus went to the heart of the matter
when he said,
"Do not be anxious,
nor troubled,
about these things.
Look at the birds of the air.
God feeds them.
Look at the lilies of the field.
God clothes them
in all their splendor.

There is not a one of us,
in spite of our best efforts,
who is dressed
so beautifully,
so splendidly,
as the red buds, the dogwoods,
and the many, many flowers
bursting
into bloom
these days.

Take a drive
through Nantahala Gorge
today.
Forget care and anxiety
as you see
what God has done!
Take time. Pause! Look
at the beautiful wild flowers
bursting into bloom
along the way.
Then consider whether or not
you have reason
to be anxious
and afraid.

Fears from Within

But there are deeper fears and anxieties
locked away
in the heart and mind
of each one of us.
A common fear is:
we are not accepted,
we are not loved.
We are lonely inside.
We live in the midst of people,
nevertheless
we are alone.

There are many who feel unwanted.
Children are often oppressed
by this fear—
the fear
that parents do not really love them.
Sometimes
these fears
are based upon reality.

There are parents who do not care,
who do not want their children.
    They are in the way!
    They are a bother!
    They cost too much!
This is sad and tragic.

Children who grow up in such
    an atmosphere,
    become adults
who run away from reality
    and from life.
They become hooked upon drugs,
    or alcohol.
Or they become addicted to sex,
    to sexual conquests.

They become warped in mind and spirit.
    For human beings need
    love and respect,
    kindness and understanding,
    strength and discipline
to become strong, courageous men
    and women.
    If this is your worry,
then you had better face up to it.
We can't run away from life,
    from ourselves,
    from our God.
The cure is not in running away.
The cure is not in hiding,
The cure is not in drowning ourselves
    in pleasure or in liquor,
    in drugs or in sex.

The cure does not even lie in surrounding
ourselves
with money and property,
with all those things
that money can buy.
Security cannot be built out of insecurity.
Yet this is the solution
we try
in one way or another.

Many try to hide their insecurity
in smoking.
They cannot manage the troubles,
the anxieties,
of the day
without this crutch.
But the so-called cure is worse
than the problem.
Take a good hard look at a bona fide case
of emphysema!
See what you are smoking up
for yourselves!

Or if we must play with the hard stuff:
drugs or acid,
because we are afraid
to face up to reality,
then go and wait upon some
of the vegetables
who tried this way.
They were once human beings, but
there is no joy,
there is no laughter.
In fact, there is no mind
to coordinate the nerves,
the muscles
the limbs,
the organs.

What would life be like,
if we had the faculties
but could not enjoy
    the beauty,
    the taste,
    the smell,
    the sound
of the world around us?

The song of a bird.
The wonder of a cloud floating
    in the sky.
The wind and the rain in our hair.
The smell of the good earth.
The taste of freshly picked strawberries.
    We could fill a book
    in short order
with the wonder, the beauty,
    of it all.
There are those who have taken
    the wrong way,
who are oblivious to all this,
who find life no longer worth living.
    Their anxieties
    have been too powerful.
They have tried to drown out
    the difficulties,
    the struggles in life.

Trust in God

What does Jesus offer us
    in the place of
    anxiety and care?
He never said that life was an easy way!
He proved by his own life that living
    in the midst of this world
    is tough.
When we stand for truth,
    for right and goodness,
    we may well end up
    on a cross.

The point is: how do we meet
the crosses,
the problems,
that come our way?
For if we live as Jesus lived
in this world,
they will surely come
to us.
Do we cringe and shrink back?
Do we compromise our convictions
about truth and right,
about love and goodness,
because these are not popular
with our friends?

Do we drift along
with the crowd
because we are lonely?
Do we get mixed up in an extra-curricular
love affair,
because it is too difficult
to make our own marriage and family
what they ought to be?
This is not what Jesus did!
Nor is this what he advocated
for those
who follow him.
It takes rigorous discipline,
self-control,
great effort,
to make of our lives
what God has intended them to be.
But it is worth every sacrifice!
for this is the good life,
the glorious life,
the life of joy,
of fulfillment.
We cannot live this life by ourselves.
We cannot live this life
without the help
of God.

Jesus demonstrated this in the garden
that night
when he wrestled
with the temptation to go his own way,
to run away and hide,
to do his own thing.
He demonstrated in his own life
that it is only when we surrender
our inner person,
our ego,
our pride,
that the power of God is available
to us.
Only then do we have the resources
to turn our anxieties,
our fears,
into positive convictions and actions.

Fears and anxieties are useless.
They have never contributed
an iota,
a jot,
to our well-being.
But 'concern' is another matter.
To have concern is healthy,
it is good
for us.
For concern grows out of love.
God's concern is for us.
He does not have a concern about himself.
Would it not be humorous
to worship a god
who was concerned about himself?
who worried and fretted
because he could not have
his own way?

No!
God's concern is for you and for me!
    He loves us.
He wants us to have a good life:
    joy,
    peace,
    and plenty.
We can have all these
    when we take God
    at his word.

Our concern is to be modeled after God.
We are to be concerned for others.
    We want them to have
    what we have.
We are moved by God to give and share,
and this we do abundantly.
    This is the good life
    under God.
A life filled with love and affection,
    with peace and joy,
    with goodness and humility,
    with giving and forgiving.
This life is ours through the grace
    of God.
Is this the life for you?

A MEDITATION UPON DEATH: A MAN HAD DIED

THE THIRD SUNDAY AFTER PENTECOST, 1977

Luke 7. 11-17

A MAN HAD DIED

A man had died:
    a young man,
    the son of a widow,
    her only son.
This is not an unusual story.
It happens all the time.
We read in the obituaries
    in the newspaper
    almost every day
that a young man has died.
Jesus must have encountered
    situations like this
    again and again.
For life expectancy was not great.
They were not trained
    in the science
    of medicine
as we are today to prolong life.
But the mortality rate is very high
    even today:
    one hundred per cent.

The only difference is
we have more years
to live than they.
But for what?
The important thing is:
how do we spend
our years?
Do we just exist?
Do we drag from one day
into the next?
Or is there some purpose,
some meaning,
to our days on earth?

A Man had Died

Death is always tragic,
unless it is relief
from suffering,
from misery,
from meaninglessness.
The death of this young man
was tragic.
His mother was a widow.
The lot of a widow
was difficult
in those days.
It was a man's world.
The woman depended upon the man
to provide
the stuff of life.

There was weeping and wailing.
Death was
hopeless.
They did not even have
a lively hope
of a resurrection
to life with God.

For a man lived on in his sons.
If there were no son,
    the family line
    came to an end.
Thus this family line was ending
    with the death
    of this son.

When the end came,
    a man went down
    to Sheol,
a dark and shadowy place.
Is there any remembrance in Sheol?
No!
    For it was not
    a real existence.
One was only a shadow
    with no substance,
    no life,
    no energy,
    no future.
So there was weeping and wailing
    when death came.

But the real tragedy of death
    is for those
    who are left behind.
Especially when the one remaining
    is dependent
    upon the departed
    for livelihood.
This is what makes this story
    so pathetic.
We can rationalize and say,
    'The dead
    are well out of it.
Their problems,
their difficulties,
their troubles,
    are at an end.'

But the troubles,
the sorrows,
the problems of the living
    remain.
Especially when death removes
    the breadwinner
    of the family.

So there was weeping and wailing!
And the weeping and wailing continues
    for days,
    for weeks,
    for months,
    for years.
Our last Newsweek has an article
    about the sorrow,
    the suffering,
    of parents
who have lost a child:
    a boy or girl,
    a teenager,
killed in an accident,
or taken by a fatal disease.

Some of us have experienced
    such tragedy.
We walk through the valley of death
    each day.
The story tells of parents
    who have left
    a son's room
just as it was the day he died.
They live through their sorrow
    each day,
    each moment of the day.
The tragedy is always
    in their consciousness.

What can we say to help them?
Can we, like Jesus, stop
    the funeral procession
    and say:
"Young man, I say to you,
    arise?"

No!
That is not within our power.
Most often we can only join
    the funeral procession,
    adding our weeping,
    our wailing,
to that of the multitude.

Death comes suddenly,
    unexpectedly,
    leaving us woebegone.
Or death comes after a long,
    a painful sickness,
    after great suffering,
    leaving us stricken.
Where is our help?
Can we call upon God
    for relief?
Does he hear our prayers
    in such a time?

Young Man, Arise!

The story in our gospel ends
    on a happy note.
Jesus came along at the right time.
    The young man
    had just died.
They were carrying him
    to his grave.
Jesus stopped the bearers.
He touched the bier.
He said,
    "Young man,
    I say to you,
    Arise!"
And the dead man sat up.
He began to speak.

How dramatic!
What wonder!
What glory!
That this young man
was brought back
to life.
Imagine for a moment the joy
that surged
through that mother's breast.
Her son was dead!
Now he was alive!
She heard him speak!
She saw him arise from the death bier!

Could anyone doubt Jesus
from that moment?
How could anyone
not believe in him?
To raise a man from the dead!
That was a wonder too great
to dismiss.
But the strange thing
about the wonder stores
in our gospels is:
They did not convince people forever
of the power of Jesus.

Multitudes did not flock to him.
His following remained a humble few.
Even their loyalty was not equal
to his death.
One betrayed him!
Another denied him!
And all the others left him
and fled!

There is something peculiar
about these stories
in our gospel.
If Jesus had such power over death,
why did he not exercise this power
more often?
He raised only two from the dead
in our gospels.
Or three, if we count Lazarus
in John's gospel.
But he must have had countless
opportunities.
Why did he not exercise his power
more often?

Why does God not exercise
his power
for us
when our loved ones are taken
by death?
Especially the young,
who have so much
to live for?
Does God not care?
Or is it better to depart this life
at a young age?
Can we find the comfort we need
in the presence of death
from such thoughts?

Death is a fearful experience
spiritually!
Death is separation from God,
the source
of life.
We are brought down to nothingness,
to non-existence.

Death is the end
    of all we hoped for,
    of all we live for.
What meaning does this story
    of the widow
    of Nain's son
    have for us?
When we are afflicted by death?

If Jesus raised only one young man
    from the dead,
this is not very helpful for us.
    One in a million,
    or a billion,
    or a trillion,
    is more the odds!
The possibility of being restored
    to life
    this side of the grave
    is very remote indeed.
Our chances are slim and none!

But perhaps this is not
    what the story
    is telling us.
And this is the point
    I would like
    to make.
This story is not intended
    to inflate us
    with the false hope
that Jesus might just chance along
    when we die,
    or when a loved one dies,
to raise us, or our loved one,
    to life!
Nor is this story intended
    to give us
    a kind of certainty
that we will be raised from the dead
    to live with God
    in his heavenly home.

What then is left to the story
to give it meaning?
Why should such a story be
in our gospel?
Unless it is intended to give us
a certain hope
that Jesus just might chance along
to give us
a few more days,
or years,
on earth?

The Meaning of the Story

This story is intended to proclaim
the gospel
to us.
The gospel which liberates us
from all
that separates us
from God.
The Apostle Paul wrote,
"Sin came into the world
through one man
and death through sin.
So death passed to all men,
for all sinned."

Death is a very real part
of life!
We live in the midst
of death!
Death brings terror to many.
It is a fearful experience for all.
We are created to live!
To live
in the presence
of God!

But how can we live in God's presence
when death robs us
of life?
and of God?
God sent his Son into the world
to deliver us from sin,
to deliver us from everything
that separates us from him!

He came to deliver us from death!
We are living in death,
without God,
without hope
in this world,
until God's Son comes to touch us!
Until he speaks his word,
"Young man,
Young woman,
I say to you,
Arise!"

Yes!
Our burdens are more than we can bear.
But through God's Son we are set free
from sin,
from death,
from the powers of evil,
so that we can live with joy,
with confidence
in this world.

How can I cope with death?
How can I cope with my sin
which brings death?
How can I cope with life itself?
I cannot, apart from
the grace of God!
For he is the one who delivers
from all fears,
from hopelessness,
from despair,
from meaninglessness in life!

For we truly come to life when he
touches us.
When he says,
"Young man,
Young woman,
I say to you,
Arise!"
Then we know the meaning of life.
Then we know the purpose for living.
There is joy and confidence,
there is hope and trust,
that our life will count
in God's great purpose
for us.

Apart from God's breathing life into us,
we are dead!
even though we may
breathe,
and move,
and eat heartily.
For life consists
of more than things,
of more than these exercises.
To be alive is to be alive in God!
To know that
each moment,
each day,
each year
is precious—a gift
of his grace.

To know that our life counts
for something,
as we use the opportunities
he gives to make an impact
for good,
for truth,
for love,
upon the lives of those about us.

Yes!
We have more days,
    more years,
to live than the young man in our lesson.
The average life span was perhaps
    forty years
    in those days.
We have sixty-five, or more!

But of what value
    are these additional days,
    and years,
if we only fritter them away
    on that which is
    of little consequence?
Of what value are those days,
    and years,
if we only live for self?
    to indulge our desires?
    to amass wealth,
    or power and fame?

Naked we came into this world!
Naked we leave it!
Death strips us
    of all our pretensions,
    of all our false hopes,
    of our wealth and property.
How vain and foolish to have these words
    written over us
    as our epitaph
when our last day has come:
    A MAN HAS DIED!

Yet that is about all
    that can be said
    for many of us.

For how has our life counted
    in the great scheme
    of things?

How great!
How moving!
How powerful
becomes the story when he touches us.
When he says,
"Young man,
Young woman,
I say to you,
Arise!"
This is what the gospel is all about!
This is why we are here!
Or at least this ought to be why
we are here.

What is the meaning of life
to us?
Do we just exist?
Do we drag from one day to the next?
Or is there some great purpose,
some rich meaning,
which marks each moment,
each day,
of our lives?

The call to God is to live!
To have a dimension
of meaning
to our lives!
Not to be the victim
of sin and death,
of selfishness and meaninglessness.
This young man must have counted
every moment,
every hour,
every day,
as a gift from God.
Life took on a deep dimension
of meaning,
of power to him.

And that is the way
    God would have it
    for us!
We were dead,
but we are alive!
We were lost,
    but we are found!
This is the glorious good news
    of the gospel!
    Every moment,
    every hour,
    every day
is a gift from God!

We have the rare privilege of sharing
    this great, good news
    with others.
What a testimony our lives should be:
    we were dead,
    but we are alive!
What joy we can bring to others.
For we can share
    this life from God
    with them.

    A man was dead.
    But he is alive!
Touched by the hand of God.
This is the eternal gospel of God.
This is the story
    of your life
    and of mine.
For the young man in our lesson is
    You!
He is
    I!

What power can death have over us?
We have been brought to life
    in God.
Death can have no power!
Unless we let death take hold
    of us
    once more.
For when our hope is in God,
    by his grace
    death is overcome
    in us.
Behold!
We were dead.
    But we are alive
    forever more!

A MEDITATION UPON A FACE

THE SIXTH SUNDAY AFTER PENTECOST, 1977

A FACE TOWARDS JERUSALEM

Luke 9. 51-61

A FACE TOWARDS JERUSALEM

There is a stone formation
in the White Mountains of New Hampshire
called
"The Great Stone Face."
It is a formation with the silhouette
of a human face
visible
even from a distance.
It is a face pointed in one direction,
firm,
unmoving,
staring into the distance year after year,
century after century.
There it is: steadfast,
unchanging
in its firm resolve,
carrying the secrets of the centuries
on its brow.
Who can know what the face has seen?
The changing landscape.
The coming of man.
Wind and weather.
All these and more have left their mark
upon the scene
around.

But the face is unchanged,
    unmoved,
    untouched
    by the scene below.
Firm in its posture.
Dedicated to the one purpose
    of looking out
    into space.

The Face of Jesus

There was a face of a man pointed
    towards Jerusalem
    long ago.
A face firm and resolute,
yet a face that could be etched
    in a smile,
    in laughter,
at the appropriate moment.
This was no ordinary man.
Yet his face hardly distinguished him
    from those
    about him.
Strangers would not have been
    unduly impressed.

For he had no form or comeliness
that we should be impressed
    by him.
Yet his face was set towards Jerusalem
    in a way
    that distinguished him.
For he had a mission,
    a calling from God,
    to fulfill.
His companions sensed the urgency,
    the resolution,
that drew him towards destiny.

What is there about this man
with his face
towards Jerusalem
that marks him off from all others?
Were there not many
in those days
with their faces towards Jerusalem?
Yes!
The roads to Jerusalem were oft crowded
with pilgrims
on their way
to the holy city.
They went up with joy and gladness
to celebrate
those sacred occasions
in the city of their fathers.

They went up again and again
to worship,
to hear
the sacred history
of God's redemptive acts,
to offer
their sacrifice
of praise and thanksgiving
to God.

But the journey of this man was
a redemptive act
in the providence of God.
He went up to offer his life
as the sacrifice
for sin.
He went up to filfill the mission
God entrusted to him
at his baptism:
to proclaim the good news of salvation
to all the people
from God.

Others went up to celebrate the feast.
He himself is
the feast
in which those who come after
partake.
Others went up to sacrifice for their sin.
He is
the sacrifice
for the sin of the world.

His face is set towards Jerusalem
with an urgency,
with a resolution,
evident to those who were
with him.
For his face was set like flint
to go to Jerusalem
and those who came after were afraid.
His face was
as firm,
as resolute
as the face on the mountain.

The Narrow Way

Jesus said to his disciples,
"Enter
by the narrow way
for the way is broad
and the gate is wide
that leads
to destruction;
and many are traveling on it.
For the gate is narrow
and the way is hard
that leads
to life
and few find it."

The way to Jerusalem was such a way:
narrow
and hard.
For the end of the way would lead
to death.
That is why there is such firmness,
such resolution,
marking his face for all to see.

God's call to follow leaves
no options
to turn to the right
or to the left.
His call is always a call to go up
to Jerusalem,
to take the way
narrow
and difficult.

Jerusalem is the holy city!
a place of destiny,
the goal of every man.
For there is God in all
his grace
and glory.
God calls everyone of us to go up
to Jerusalem;
to walk this way
narrow and hard
that leads to life.

Yes!
There is something magnificent
about that face
towards Jerusalem,
pointed in one direction,
unmoved
to turn aside
by the attractions visible
to the view.

What concentration!
What determination!
What dedication!
the journey to Jerusalem demands.
There are easier ways.
There are more attractive ways.
There are ways that take less
in sacrifice,
that promise instant
and greater rewards.

He who takes this way
must indeed be under the compulsion
of God!
When the days drew near for Jesus
to be received up,
he set his face to go up
to Jerusalem.
This is a veiled reference
to the cross
that awaited Jesus
at the end of this journey.

His mission could only be accomplished
through his dying
for the sins of the world.
This is what marks off his journey
to Jerusalem
from any other.
His journey is touched
by a sense of drama,
of tragedy,
yet of life's fulfillment
that life awaits him
in the holy city.

There is courage,
there is daring,
there is love
 on that face:
love for the lost,
 the hopeless,
 the despairing.
Love for the loveless,
 for those neglected,
 forsaken by man.
Love for the outsiders,
 for the rejected,
 for the sinner.

But there is aloneness too.
For the face towards Jerusalem is
 a lonely face.
For who understands?
Who is willing to travel that way
 with him?
He was despised and rejected
 by men,
 a man of sorrows
 and acquainted with grief.

He sent messengers ahead,
 who went,
 who entered
a village of the Samaritans,
 to make ready for him.
But the people would not receive him,
 for his face was set
 towards Jerusalem.

Who wants to receive the one
 whose face is
 towards Jerusalem?
Who walks the narrow road?
Who is determined to fulfill
 the will of God
 at all costs?

And it costs to go to Jerusalem!
Friend and family,
Dear ones who do not understand,
who are not committed
with that same fervor,
with that sense of mission.

Yes!
It is a narrow road,
the way of obedience,
the way of fulfillment,
the way of service.
But he who walks that way,
does not walk alone,
for he walks with God.
From whence did Jesus draw his courage?
his resolution?
on that way, if not from God?

Our Face Towards Jerusalem

The road to Jerusalem is his way
to walk.
No one could walk it for him.
For God called him
to a mission,
to a destiny,
that was his alone to fulfill.

Yet the road is for everyman!
It is the road
for you and me.
For God has called you
and God has called me
to a mission,
to a destiny,
that only you and I can fulfill.

No one can walk that road for us.
Each one must walk it for himself.
    The determination,
    the resolution,
    the firmness
that marks our face on the road
    to Jerusalem
    is not different from his.
For when the hand of God is laid
    upon us,
we too have a mission,
a God-given mission,
    which can only be fulfilled
    by each one for himself.

Jesus walked that way before us.
He opened the way so that each one of us
    can follow
    in his footsteps.
But how do we walk that way?
    Are we like those
    filled with empty resolutions,
who saw him on the way and said,
    "I will follow you
    wherever you go?"

Promises come easily to our lips.
We want to be where the action is,
    but we do not want
    too much action
    for ourselves.
How readily we have said,
    "I will follow you, Lord!"
    and yet we have to make
    our first move.
For our following has been puny indeed!

There have been words but no action.
Beautiful thoughts,
wonderful idealism,
but far from the realities of life.
It is easy
to sit in the pew
and let resolutions come to mind.
But it is so difficult,
oh, so difficult,
to carry them
forward in life.

Pew Christianity is indeed the easy way!
Here our thoughts are often filled
with beautiful sentiments.
Here we often make
the easy promise.
But out in life, confronted
by those who will not receive
the Christ.
ridiculed by friends and family,
it is so difficult
to put these sentiments
to work.

One said to Jesus,
"I will follow you, Lord;
but let me first say farewell
to those at home."
Loyalty to family, loyalty to friends,
can be the first obstacle
on the journey
to Jerusalem.

What is our mission in life?
What is our calling from God?
Do we know?
Have we let the voice of God
probe our hearts?

Has he sorted out for us
    where our treasure
    lies in life?
Is it his kingdom and his righteousness?
Or is there something, someone,
    dearer to our hearts?
    Something, someone
promising more immediate rewards?

How difficult it is for us
    to understand,
    to know,
that though we may earn our bread
    by selling merchandise,
    or building buildings,
    or making merchandise,
    or keeping books,
    or washing dishes,
    or teaching children,
that God has a mission reserved
    for each one of us,
    and only for each one of us!

It is the worship of God,
but it is more than
    the worship of God.
It is supporting the work of the kingdom
    with our gifts,
but it is more than
    supporting the kingdom
    with our gifts.
It is being a student of the word of God,
but it is more than
    being a student
    of the word of God.

It is the face set
towards Jerusalem!
It is the resolution to walk
in God's way,
that narrow,
that difficult way,
even when the crowd is headed
in the other
direction.

The moral life,
the life of integrity,
the life of purity,
is a lonely way, for few walk
upon it.
But it is the way God calls us
to walk.
It is the way of the face
towards Jerusalem.

It is the way of giving ourselves
to others;
of expending our lives in witness
to others
of the grace of God in our lives.
For we are all called
with a sacred calling
to be Christs to one another:
to bear the burdens of the weak,
to help the infirm,
to be the eyes for the blind.

It is to be strong in God
in the time of crisis.
It is not to permit
the tragedies of life,
the inconstancy of friends,
the cruelty of any man,
determine the direction, the set
of our face.

Our face may be like
    the great stone face
    etched in rock
    in the mountains of New Hampshire.
But for what purpose?
What is the meaning, the service,
    of such a face?
Or our face may be like
    the face of Jesus,
    set steadfastly,
    set resolutely,
towards Jerusalem.

Walking the way God would have us go.
Fulfilling the mission that
    only you,
    or only I,
can fulfill by the grace of God.
    Saying his words,
    doing his deeds,
    loving and forgiving,
even as he loves and forgives us.

There was the face of a man
    pointed
    towards Jerusalem
    long ago!
There is the face of a man, a woman,
    pointed
    towards Jerusalem,
    today!
Can that face be yours?
Can that face be mine?
    Yes!
    By the grace of God!

A MEDITATION ON LOINS AND LAMPS

THE TWELFTH SUNDAY
AFTER PENTECOST,
1977

GIRDED LOINS AND BURNING LAMPS

Luke 12. 32-40

GIRDED LOINS AND BURNING LAMPS

Some years ago a tire company
 advertised
 their products
with the picture of a sleepy boy
 in night attire
 carrying
 a lighted candle.
The caption read,
 "Time to retire."
It was clever publicity,
 appropriate
for their product.

Jesus said,
 "Let your loins be girded
 and your lamps burning."
Here are two metaphors
which seem to be in contradiction.
 Burning lamps
are for the nighttime.
 Girded loins
are for the day's march.

Long ago
in Egypt land
God gave this command
to a slave people:
"Take a lamb without blemish;
kill your lamb in the evening,
sprinkle the blood upon the doorposts.
Then shall you eat
the flesh that night,
roasted.
In this manner you shall eat it:
your loins girded,
your sandals on your feet,
your staff in your hand.
You shall eat it in haste."

On the Way to the Promised Land

Why such instructions?
Because they were to march out of Egypt
that night.
They were on their way
to the land of promise,
to the land God
would show them.
Girded loins and burning lamps!
These are the marching attire
for the people of God.

God's people are always on the march
to the land of promise.
We do not put down our roots
as if we shall be here
forever.
Not when we belong to the company
of God's people.
The land of promise is still before us!
We are under orders to be on the march
for God!

Christian people are to be awake,
alert!
ready
to move out at the command of God!
Awake,
alert!
to the time on God's calendar.

Jesus said,
"Blessed are those servants
whom the master finds awake
when he comes.
You must be ready!
For the Son of man is coming
at an unexpected hour."

Whatever the state of our existence,
whatever progress we have made
towards our goals,
we have not yet arrived
at the place where God would have us.

For the Kingdom of God is not yet!
The Kingdom of God is here;
yet it is not yet
all that it shall be!
We may have made progress,
there may have been self-improvement
in our lives.
But we have not yet arrived,
we are not yet perfect.
Therefore let us press on
towards the goal
God has set before us.

Time to retire?
Never, for the people of God.
Our symbols—
Girded loins
and burning lamps.
These are symbols of readiness
for what lies ahead.
Girded loins!
Because there is a hard march
for the people of God.

Our journey is not an easy way,
    over paved roads
    with a chart
    mapped out by a travel agency.
No!
We enter into the unknown
    on uncharted paths.
We go where others have not gone
    before us.
For all who march out of Egypt land
    strike out
    into the uncharted wilderness.

    Burning lamps!
Because there is darkness ahead;
    darkness
    which must be lighted up
by the presence of the living God.
Wherever we march on the uncharted paths,
    there is God
    in the pillar of cloud
    and the flaming fire.
We march.
But we do not go alone.

We march in a great company:
    in the company of all
    who have responded
    to the call of God.
In the company of all
    who seek
    the promised land.
We are beset by the perils
    of the night.
There are enemies who threaten,
    who would keep us
    from the promised land.

But we hear the words of our Lord
ringing in our ears:
"Fear not!
little flock.
It is your Father's good pleasure
to give you the kingdom."

Israel came out of Egypt,
demoralized,
fearful.
Before them was the wilderness,
the great unknown.
How could they survive the long,
the arduous march?

Where would their leader take them?
Away from whatever comforts,
whatever security
they had known.
There was grinding toil,
the whips
of their masters.
But even that was more attractive,
more appealing,
than a trackless wilderness,
an unknown future.

The Present State

There is always temptation
to settle down
where we are,
as if we were already
in the land of promise.
The world is always so good
where we are.
Perhaps our lot is not great.
Perhaps there is grinding toil,
the orders
of the taskmasters.
But we are content!

Girded loins and burning lamps?
They are meaningless to all
    who have their feet planted
    where they are.
To all who cannot hear
    the voice of God.
To all who say,
    This land is good.
    Let us build here.
This is the promised land.

Yes!
We are shortsighted. The treasures
    of the world are dear
    to us.
Many will not exchange them
    for the Kingdom.
    Our life is here.
    Our future is here.
There is nothing beyond
    what we hold
    in our hand.
Show me the treasures of heaven.
I will show you the treasures
    that have more substance,
    more meaning,
for my life here and now.

    Girded loins!
    Burning lamps!
Are these the symbols of the people
    of God?
Are the people of God on the march
    today?
Where do the people of God
    make their presence
    known?

I looked in the marketplace
    and, lo, the people of God
    were not there!
It was each for himself
and the devil take the hindmost.
    The great god
    of the marketplace
    was money,
    treasure.
And there was no room for God.

I looked in the halls of government
    and, lo, the people of God
    were not there!
For here the password was power:
Power to write the laws of the land
    to favor the rich,
    those of influence
    at the top of society.
Power to call justice
    whatever suited
    their fancy.
Power to keep the poor,
    poor and subservient.
And there was no room for God.

I looked in the halls of learning
    and, lo, the people of God
    were not there!
For here the keynote was intellect,
    wisdom,
    a rational approach
    to life.
Who needs God? they say.
For man is the measure of all things.
    Man is the master
    of his fate,
    the captain of his soul.
And there was no room for God.

I looked in the great centers of art
and, lo, the people of God
were not there!
For the discord, the disharmony,
attested the emptiness
of man's soul.
And there was no room for God!

I looked among the people
and, lo, God was not there!
Lives devoted to meaninglessness,
to empty pleasures.
The idols before which they bow—
an Elvis Presley,
a Joe Namath,
a Farrah Fawcett-Majors.
And there was no room for God!

I looked in the churches
and, lo, God was not there!
For who listens to the voice of God
today?
Church leaders devoted to numbers,
to proper attire,
to statistics,
to many resolutions.
Church people devoted
to their own interests.
And there was no room for God!

Who is on the way to the land of promise?
Who hears the voice of the master?
"Lay not up for yourselves
treasures on earth
where moth and rust consume,
where thieves break through and steal."
Jesus laid his finger on the heart
of man's desire
when he said,
"Where your treasure is,
there will your heart be also."

Girded Loins and Burning Lamps

Girded loins,
Burning lamps
are not our symbols.
But they are to be!
For Jesus said and he says today,
"Let your loins be girded
and your lamps burning."
Be like men who are waiting
for their master
to come home!

Remain not in Egypt!
Among the fleshpots.
Go forth on your way
to the land of promise!
And where is this land of promise
of which he speaks?
Is it heaven we seek?
Yes and no!
The land of promise is not
pie in the sky
by and by.

What is being a Christian to many?
It is the promise of heaven in the end.
Be good boys and girls now.
God will reward you in the end.
And what is this goodness? It is
white shirts and ties,
correctness and propriety,
walking the straight and narrow,
not swearing, stealing, or whoring,
keeping one's nose out of other
people's business,
belonging to the right crowd,
being respectable and respected,
doing our deeds of charity for all
to see,
so that we receive the proper credit
from men.

But this is a far cry
from the word of the Master who said,
"Let your loins be girded,
your lamps burning;
and be like men
who are waiting for their master
to come home."

The body of believers is always
a marching body,
under orders
from the leader.
Go out and possess the land!
Take possession of the people
in the name of God!
Bear witness to the grace of God
in your life!
Tell the people that God
has set you free
from bondage
to selfishness and self-centeredness.
Declare that there is one Lord,
one Master, of life:
not money, not pleasure,
not family, not power,
not even the church.
For God has sent his Son to deliver you,
to set you free
from a life of no purpose.
For what purpose is there to life,
if we only seek
to have heaven
in the end?

Girded loins,
Burning lamps,
crying out for commitment:
commitment not to self,

not to satisfying one's own desires,
to building up
security
upon this world's goods.

    Girded loins,
    Burning lamps!
These are the symbols of the people of God:
    a people
    committed to his purpose
    to bring all the peoples
    of the earth
together into one great family.

    A family
    devoted
to truth, goodness, love.
    A people
    dedicated
to the good each of the other.
    A people
    on the march
to bring the gospel into all the world.

    What is the gospel?
    It is good news!
But not just that we will have heaven
    in the end.
No!
It is the good news that
    we are set free
    from the shackles
    of selfishness,
    of selfhood,
so that we might serve the living God.

It is feeding the hungry,
    clothing the naked,
    ministering to the sick,
    to the helpless,
    bearing the burdens of the weak,
    in the name of Jesus.
It is walking
    in the footsteps of Jesus,
    showing compassion,
    kindness and love.

It is knowing the truth
and seeking the truth
with dedication and purpose.
It is living a life of integrity,
of honesty,
being pure and chaste
in our words and deeds,
not because the Lord may come
at an unexpected time
and catch us
where we ought not to be.

It is this: the people of God
are on the march,
on their way
to the land of service,
where the people are.
The people who need God.
People in bondage
to self and money,
to pleasure and power.
In bondage to a hundred gods
that are like
a monkey on their backs.

Gods that are slave masters,
who bring death
and destruction
in the end.
For all the gods of the land
cannot save us.

Girded loins,
and burning lamps!
He is the God who saves,
who calls us to a life of service.
Who lays out the land before us:
the land of fulfillment,
the land of promise.
136 A land in which each of us can come
into his own
A land of promise,
for we can grow in the image,
and likeness
of our God.

      Our lives
      shaped and molded
      by his hand
according to the pattern, the model,
      which we see
      in Christ our Lord.

And though we are beset
      by fierce enemies
      on this journey,
enemies who are determined to cast
      God from his throne
      and destroy him,
we do not hesitate or fear.
For he said,
     "Fear not, little flock!
It is your Father's good pleasure
      to give you the kingdom."

      Girded loins,
      and burning lamps!
Here is our password
      to the land of promise,
      to the city of God.
      And is not there somewhere.
      It is here
      before us!
Out in the streets,
      the highways,
      the byways of life
where the people are:
      the people
      who cry out
      for God.

A MEDITATION ON BLINDNESS

THE TWENTY—THIRD SUNDAY AFTER PENTECOST, 1976

BLIND BARTIMAEUS

Mark 10. 46-52

BLIND BARTIMAEUS

Blindness! A most severe handicap
    for a human
    to endure.
There must be tens of thousands
    of blind persons
    in our land.

How would it be to grope in darkness?
Never to see
    the light of day,
    the glorious sunset,
    the multicolored hillsides in autumn,
    the birds in flight,
    the fish darting in the stream,
    the gaily colored flowers nodding in the breeze,
    the face of a friend,
    the dimpled smile of a little child?

Yet the blind adjust to darkness.
They find their way
    through the maze of life.

They hear music and laughter.
They know love and friendship too.

John Milton wrote a poem ON HIS BLINDNESS:

"When I consider how my light is spent
Ere half my days in this dark world and wide,
And that one talent which is death to hide
Lodged with me useless, though my soul more bent
To serve therewith my Maker, and present
My true account, lest He returning chide;
'Doth God exact day labor, light denied?'
I fondly ask. But Patience, to prevent
That murmur, soon replies, 'God doth not need
Either man's work or his own gifts. Who best
Bear his mild yoke, they serve him best. His state
Is kingly: thousands at his bidding speed,
And post o'er land and ocean without rest;
They also serve who only stand and wait'."

Blindness need not be
the handicap
we make it.
For in our blindness
we can see God.

A Blind Man

There was a blind man seated
by the roadside
one day.
We do not even know his name.
He is called Bartimaeus,
the son of Timaeus.

He is nameless:
he is every man,
everyone who has never
seen God.
God in his loveliness,
his beauty,
his glory.

For the number of those
who have not seen God
is like the sand
on the seashore.

Do we see God?
No!
We are like blind Bartimaeus,
    waiting by the side of the road
    for light to come.
Light to pierce the darkness of our night.
Light to lift the darkness
    of despair,
    of anguish,
    of suffering and dread.

How can we be useful when we cannot see:
When the light of day is shrouded
    to our sight?
When we must grope our way uncertainly
    through uncharted paths?
What is it that we seek in life?
Is it only the fulfillment
    of our dreams of riches,
    of fame and power?
Or do we only wait by the side of the road,
    marking time
    till our last day
    is spent?

Is life made up for us
    out of the good,
    the noble,
    the true?
Is there love within
    that kindles
    the flame
    of personhood?
Do we find truth and freedom,
    the joy of being alive?
    sharing our strength,
    our sympathy,
    our love
    with others?
with those who have not?

Do we fritter away the moments,
the days,
the years
by the side of the road
because there has been no great challenge,
no great cause,
that has enlisted
our support?

Bartimaeus was like that—
waiting,
waiting interminably,
as the days and years rolled by.
And he in darknes!
Waiting for one to lift
the mantle of night,
so that the day
might shine through.

How precious the moments!
Yet how uselessly they are spent
by the side of the road,
marking time
according to the cadence, the rhythms,
of the world out there.
Waiting while the precious opportunities
pass us by—
Opportunities to bring
a smile,
a ray of sunshine,
into the life of someone sorely pressed
on every side
by the burdens,
by the cares of life.

Bartimeaus!
Why do you wait by the side of the road?

Why do you uselessly use up
the time,
the precious time,
God has allotted you?

Can it be that all there is to life is
    to sit and wait?
Is this the purpose of God
    for you?
Can it be that God created
    you
    only to sit
    and wait?

Bartimaeus!
You are everyman!
You are every one of us!
    You are I
    and I am you.
For what do we do
    but wait in darkness
    when there is light?

Sitting in lonesomeness,
    in self-pity,
mourning our dismal past,
    our dismal present,
    our hopeless future.
For can tomorrow be more than today?

The darkness, the crushing darkness,
    has been with me
    all my days.
What is light?
What can light be
    to those
    who have never known
    light?
Can life be more than waiting
    by the side of the road?
    Helpless?
    Seeking help
    where there is none?
Can it be that there is more to life
    than I find here
    by the side of the road?

The Man On The Road

Hark!
What is the sound I hear?
    A footfall?
Yes!
The footfalls of a great multitude,
    a great host of men,
    of women and children.
The footfalls of those who walk
    with certain step.
Who march along,
    not stumbling,
    not falling,
following the man in the lead.

Who is that man
Whose firm tread upon the path of life
has shaken many
    out of lethargy,
    out of despair?
That man who has brought light—
    light
    that has pierced
    the darkness of night
    that shrouds our sight?
Who is he?
He is Jesus of Nazareth!
A man from God, who came to give sight,
    to bring light,
    to blind Bartimaeus
    by the side of the road.

We wait by the side of the road
    in our blindness
    until he comes.
We cannot hasten his coming.
Yet he is here,
    in that moment
    when we least expect him.

When all seems hopeless and lost,
    when despair
    and deep darkness smother us,
    He comes.
For in the fullness of time
God sent forth his Son.

The waiting has been for long.
Yet it is not in vain.
For God knows
    our darkness,
    the gloom and despair
    that weighs heavily
    upon all mankind.
He will not leave us in darkness.
    He comes!
    He is here!
Even as we wait by the side of the road,
    that man
    draws near.
That man we call Jesus of Nazareth.

He comes to open the eyes of the blind.
To lift the veil that shrouds us
    from God.
So that we might see him.
So that we might know him—
    the God of truth
    of righteousness,
    of love.
Without him we cannot see God.
We cannot know God until the darkness
    is lifted
    from our dim eyes.
How do we know God?
We see him in that man Jesus.
That man who comes to us
    as we wait
    in our blindness
    by the side of the road.

Yes!
We shrink back from the glory
    of his presence,
    unaccustomed as we are
to light and truth and glory.

Yet we cannot let him pass us by.
There is a magnetism that draws us
    even though we
    would turn away.
There are men who love
    darkness
    rather than light.
Men who have been touched
    by the light
    of God's presence.
Men who have turned back
    into darkness
    and gloom.

Turned back
    to their own business
    by the side of the road!
Unwilling
    to let the light shine
    into their hearts,
    into their minds!
How can we be blind to God?
How can we turn from him?
It takes effort
    to deny God,
    to deny his presence,
    his power
in this world and in our lives.

There are many Bartimaeus's
By the side of the road;
blind men
who will always be blind.
Blind! Because they will not look
to that man
on the road—
that man Jesus!
That man from God
who came
to heal our blindness,
to let the light of God
shine into the deepest recesses
of our selves.

Are you such a one?
Would you remain in darkness
because you have
no time for God?
Is your darkness
a joy,
a pleasure,
so that you would not exchange it
for the light of God?

Yes!
There are those
who love darkness
rather than light!
Can it be you?
Can it be I?
Or are we like the Bartimaeus
of our lesson?
The Bartimaeus
who sprang to his feet,
who threw off his mantle,
who came to Jesus?
The man Bartimaeus
who cried and cried,
"Jesus,
Son of David,
have mercy on me!"

Seeing Bartimaeus

The touch of his hand,
the sound of his voice,
    gives light.
He comes from the God
who in the beginning said,
    Let there be light!
    And there was light.
So in our lives there is light:
    the light
    of the presence
    of the glory of God.

Now the road lies before us.
Our eyes are opened so that
    we can see
    the way we are to go.
If we do not use the gift of sight
    which he brings us,
would it not be better
    to sit
    by the side of the road
    in darkness?

No!
The road leads upward and onward,
    the way
    we are to go.
And there is the man Jesus in the lead,
    pointing us
    the way
    we are to go.
The roadside is lined by the many
    who wait—waiting
    for the sound of his voice,
    for the touch of his hand,
    for the light of God's presence
to lift the mantle of darkness
    which overshadows us.

There they are,
    as we were,
    waiting,
    many in hopelessness
    and despair.
For so many nights have passed
    without light.
What joy!
What grace from God
    that now we see.
We were in darkness,
    but now we see.

Oh, the wonder,
the glory of it all!
    We were blind,
    but now we see.
But we see more than God.
We see the faces
    of those along the way;
the faces
    of those waiting
    for the gift of sight.
Waiting for
    the knowledge of God.

Ah, now we know
    why God came to us
    by the side of the road
    in this man
    Jesus of Nazareth!
It is that we might walk
    in his footsteps,
so that God might leave
    the imprint
    of his life
    on others through us.

No longer are we
Bartimaeus
        by the side of the road.
We are
Bartimaeus
        on the road with him,
        treading
        where his feet
        have trod.
Bringing the light of the glory of God
        to those
        who do not know him.
Proclaiming the great glad news
        to all
        who sit in darkness.

Behold, the people who sat in darkness
        have seen a great light.
And for those who sat
        in the shadow of death,
        light has dawned.

POETIC MUSINGS

OUR YEARS

The years have rolled along
Leaving their mark upon us.
    The growth,
    The scars,
The unfilled wishes and desires.
What of the hopes and aspirations
    That animated us
    In youth!
We faced the future with confidence
    That the world
    Out there
    Would be ours,
Subject to our whims and desires.

Have the years only passed us by?
Have we only existed?
Lived from moment to moment
    Without purpose?
Have we failed to strive toward the ideals,
    The ambitions,
    The hopes
That once fired our resolve?
Have we only lived to serve self
    And selfish ambition?
God forbid that we spend ourselves so cheaply!

And now as we come to the best of our years
Is there joy and gratitude and hope
    That the future before us
    Is greater than the past?
Greater than all we envisioned in our youth?
That there is meaning, purpose,
    Strength of mind and body,
    Strength of spirit,
    To share with one another.
To realize a fulfillment
Greater than we could have hoped or dreamed.

O God, who has guided us through the years,
Let joy and peace and blessednes
    Radiate from us
    Into the lives
    Of those about us.
Let all that we have experienced be shared
    To strengthen,
    To ennoble
The children of men.
So that when our last day is at hand
We may know that our years have been filled
    With richness and goodness
    For us
    And for all that you have made.
That all we have touched has been ennobled
Because we fulfilled our years on earth.

WHO AM I?

Who says I am not the one I once was?
Am I less or am I more?
Has life passed me by
Without leaving its imprint upon me?
    Unscarred,
    Unblemished,
By encounter with others,
By challenge of calling,
By marks of suffering?

No! All of life is caught up in this person
    At this moment
    Here am I!
A part of all that I have met
Shaped and molded
    By circumstance,
    By friend and foe,
    By inner thoughts and desires,
    To be a new 'I';
An 'I' greater than I could have been
    Left to myself.

The hand of God is in my life
For he has captured me to be his own.
He has lifted me out of
    Selfishness
    And vanity
To a great concern,
A great love for others.
Who am I?
One who has drunk deeply from the many sides of life—
    The mountain heights of music,
    The deep wells of artistic creation,
    The glorious phrasings of the masters of the word.

O God! What beauty you have shared with me:
    Life
    Strength
    Creative imagination
    The zest for being.
My cup is filled to overflowing with goodness and joy.
Help me to be what I ought to be,
To find my place within the family of your people,
    To share
    All of me
With you
And with one another.
Who am I? Your handiwork
    Shaped forever
    And formed in the lives of those
    Who come after.

OUR TOMORROWS

Our future is fraught with mystery,
    It is the unknown.
We cannot enter into it until tomorrow.
Yet our tomorrows are ever before us;
    We never reach them
    For we live today.

What do our tomorrows bring?
    Seldom what we expect;
Sometimes more, sometimes less,
Always the wonder of surprise.
There's the great, glad joy of triumph,
    Of reaching goals long striven for.
There is failure—
The hard truth of knowing some things
    Are beyond our reach.

There are small expectations
    And little consequences.
There is toil and drudgery,
The excitement of the spectacular.
There is turmoil and quietness,
    The sharing of ourselves with others,
    Our thoughts, our life;
Entering into the pain of one another
    And of our own.

There is the joy and gladness of new birth
    And new life.
There is love—
The great glad tumultuous feeling
    Of being one with another.
So we enter into our tomorrows
    With confidence and joy,
Knowing that no pain or anguish
Can rob us of the peace
    Which passes all understanding.

Our tomorrows belong to God
    Who made us;
Who gives life and breath and every good.
How can we be downcast and overthrown
    When trouble comes?
No, our life is in God
Who has brought us to this day
    And into our tomorrows
    With the promise of his presence.

Our future is in God
    Who turns our tomorrows into good;
Who saves us from loneliness and despair,
From anxiety and fear
With the good news that our tomorrows belong to him,
    That our future is sure;
So that leaning into our tomorows
We have strength for this day
To carry the burdens of today with the certain hope
That our tomorrows will be rich in blessing
    For all who walk with God.

OUR LIFE

Our life is in the hand of God
    Who made us,
Shaped and molded to be his own,
To live in a good land;
To know the peace and confidence
    Of his presence:
To live in trust that his will
    Is good and gracious.

Our life is in the hand of God:
    What wonder in that word!
Made to be little lower than the angels,
Crowned with glory and honor,
    Blessed with his presence;
Called to worship him,
To serve the children of men
    In word and thought and deed.

Our life is in the hand of God:
How can care and anxious fear fret me,
Rob me of quietness and strength
    With God beside me.
I place my hand in his
And enter boldly into the tomorrows,
Knowing that his grace sustains
    And keeps me from all evil.

Our life is in the hand of God:
I cannot be overthrown,
Cast down by fickle fate,
    Trouble, or suffering;
For my destiny belongs to him.
My future is sure,
He promises life, the abundant life,
    To all who trust in him.

THE DOOR

What lies beyond the door?
Shall I open it and see?
Why do I hesitate?
What do I fear?
    New experiences?
    Strange places?
Why this foreboding in my heart?

Does this door open upon a peaceful scene?
A quiet idyllic glen?
Where all is sunshine and roses,
    The bird's call,
    The dog's bark,
The sun shimmering on the fen?

Does this door open upon a storm cloud?
A fierce and perilous place?
Where all is darkness and gloom,
    The wind's blast
    The hail's beat,
A shadow on a face?

What lies beyond this door?
What is there for me?
Is it peace and contentment?
    The fulfillment
    Of my hopes and dreams?
Or is it disillusion,
    Conflict,
    Strife?
How can I know until I open the door to see?

I will open the door.
I will not flee.
For life belongs to courage,
To those who dare to be.

TO A ROSE

How lovely your fragrance,
little Rose;
Bearing the essence of heaven in your bosom.
How fragrant your aroma with sweet odors
Lovely
Above all
Under heaven.
What joy you inspire in the heart of a maid,
Poignant
Fleeting-
Of love unending.

How exquisite your beauty,
little Rose;
Unfolding in myriad layers of velvet.
How delicate your petals
With color
Unmatched
In all creation.
What hope you impart to the heart of a maid,
Ennobling—
Speaking
Of life unending.

A TREE

Bright and glorious are the trees
Shining in the autumn breeze,
There they stand in all their splendor,
Colors telling of God's wonder,
Gracious gifts from God above,
Who made all things in his love.

Soon they'll lift their arms in prayer
Stripped of all their glory, bare,
In their starkness we will see
The true nature of a tree,
Barren limbs against the sky,
Sing their praise to God on high.

When we stand before our Lord
With our hearts and thoughts outpoured,
We are like that tree so barren,
Stripped of all our pride, uncaring,
Praying God that we may be
Fashioned like that glorious tree.

(Can be sung to *DEJLIG ER DEN HIMMEL BLAA*
No. 75 in the LUTHERAN BOOK OF WORSHIP)

TO MOTHER

Be fruitful and multiply, said God.
So mothers came to be
Created by the Creator to bear life,
To nurture each new generation in the ways
    Of truth and goodness,
    Of love and peace.

What would I be without mother?
What would you be?
My life, your life,
    Shaped,
    Molded
    At mother's knee;
Introduced to each new experience in life,
Protected, sheltered, loved.

How good it was to feel the warmth
    Of mother's arms;
    Comforted
    Encouraged,
Strengthened for our encounter
With the world out there.

How can I forget you, Mother,
    On this day set apart for you?
    Your devotion,
    Your love,
    Your tender care.
What would I be without you, Mother?
Not the one I am
But someone less;
Perhaps unfit for life,
    Untempered,
    Untrue;
Living for self and selfish ambition.

But you opened a world to me,
A world alive with beauty;
A world of people in need
    Of compassion
    And love.
A challenging world demanding the best of me;
Calling me to serve God
    And the children of men
    With my life, my heart, my all.

Mother, how can I return all you are to me?
How can I live up to your hopes,
    Your prayers?
Fulfilling the expectations, the dreams,
That move a mother's heart?
I can live as you would have me live,
Following the paths into which you led me
    In childhood
    And in youth;
Living for truth, for beauty and goodness,
Loving as you have loved me.

O God, the source of life,
The giver of every good and perfect gift;
    How infinitely wise
To form this cradle for our being;
To give us mothers patterned after
    Your own Father love.
What joy that on this day
We can thank you for Mother!

THE VINE AND THE BRANCH

Jesus said, "You are a branch,
    A branch of the vine;
You cannot bear fruit without me."
What does he mean by this word?
Why without him can I not be?

God is the Creator God
    Who gives life to all—
Shaping man out of the dust of the ground,
Breathing into him the breath of life,
    So man became a living soul,
Shaped and molded to have life in God,
    To live in harmony with him.

But man turned from God
    To go his own way;
Denied the source of life and power
To live out of his own resources.
The branch said to the vine,
"You are not my father."
So the branch became fruitless,
    Withered and died;
Bearing another fruit than God intended.

What did God do?
Did he cast off the branch forever?
He planted another stump,
A root in the dry ground;
A root which sprouted and grew
Bringing forth new branches
    Grafted into the life of God.

That branch is Christ
Who gave his life to give life to all;
Who came to bring us to God
To restore us to the life man once knew.
But life is fragile,
In peril at every moment from every side,
    Exposed to danger,
    Threatened,
Needing the tender care of the Giver of life.

God creates and recreates
    Always to be his own;
So that abiding in him
We might reach the end,
    The fulfillment
    Of why we came to be.
"Go and bear fruit," said the Lord,
"Fruit that is pleasing to me.
Love one another even as I have loved you."

Love is of God, for God is love;
We cannot love except he abides in us,
Engrafting his self, his nature,
    Into our being.
We are turned inward upon our selves,
Seeking our own in all we do
    Until God turns us,
Lifting us out of self-interest,
    And selfishness,
To look upon one another as neighbor,
    Brother, sister, friend.

What joy that God invites us to share
    His life, his love;
    To become like him,
Shaped in the image of Christ his Son,
Living as he lived in the world,
    Loving as he loved;
Branches growing forth from the vine,
    Abiding in him.

LOVE ONE ANOTHER

Love one another as I have loved you,
    said Jesus;
This is a large order for man to fill.
What is the measure of the Jesus' love?
It is a cross
    Where he gave his life,
Not for self but for others,
    To bring us to God.

The cross is a brutal, shameful death
    Made for sinners,
For those who defy God and man,
Have no respect for life or limb,
Who rob and steal and kill
    To have their way.
But Jesus did none of these.
    He came from God
To teach God's way with power,
The way of truth and right and goodness;
To do the works of God,
Works of compassion, kindness and love;
He lived, he died for others.

To give one's life for a good man is noble,
To die for a friend commendable,
But to give one's life for the enemy
Is beyond the measure of our love.
Yet he says, Love one another
As I have loved you.
Does he mean that we are to give our lives
For the stranger?
For the bad?
For those who hate?
Yes, we are to become as he was in the world,
Taking thought for the needs of others,
Giving and sharing of our substance,
Of our life, that others
May find the way to God.

The measure of our love is his love,
Loving the unlovely;
Walking in their footsteps,
Feeling their pain.
It is a cup of cold water for the thirsty,
Bread for the hungry,
A cloak for the naked;
It is living with sinners,
With those despised and cast out.
Sharing hospitality with strangers,
Giving our life for their good.

It is taking up the cross,
Bearing the burdens of the brokenhearted,
Dying that others may live.
How can we love in this measure?
How can we fulfill our call?
Only as the Jesus' love is planted
Deep in our being,
Can we give ourselves to others.
Let us ask for this favor
That God may come with power,
Shaping and molding us in the Jesus' image
To love even as he loved all.

www.ingramcontent.com/pod-product-compliance
Lightning Source LLC
LaVergne TN
LVHW050644100826
845148LV00011B/1975

* 9 7 8 1 7 2 5 2 8 7 7 8 5 *